T **S**

A pr **ng**

R

This book is to be returned on or before the date above.
It may be borrowed for a further period if not in demand.

Essex County Council

Essex County
Council Libraries

Training Skills by Jason De Boer

ISBN 978-0-9553088-7-1

Originally published in ebook format in 2006 by my-skills limited
First published in print format in 2007 by my-skills limited
For further information please visit us online at www.my-skills.co.uk
Telephone and Fax +44 (0)1484 649565

© 2007 my-skills limited

Printed in Great Britain by CPI Antony Rowe Limited, Chippenham

my-skills limited
Registered as a private limited company in England
Company No. 5713998

Contents

Preface

Training is an increasingly important aspect of many jobs across a broad range of sectors, both private and public. It can encompass a variety of activities from formal training courses and induction programmes for new hires, through to informal coaching and mentoring by managers and experienced colleagues. Underpinning all of these activities is a core set of skills and tools, based on established best practices and academic research.

This book is designed to provide a **quick, accessible and practical introduction** to these skills and tools, whether you are a new trainer looking to design and deliver a training programme for the first time, a manager looking to organize training for your team members, or someone working in another field who is considering training as a career change.

The structure of this book broadly follows that of a number of recognized training qualifications, including the **CIPD Certificate in Training Practice**, which is widely recognized and highly sought after by employers across a broad spectrum of industry sectors.

Using this book on its own may not qualify you as a trainer, but it will certainly provide you with a good understanding of the skills and tools required. It will give you a flavour of training as a career, and it will provide you with a head start should you decide to study for a formal training qualification. This book can also be used as a revision guide and refresher for people already studying for a training qualification. Details on how to obtain further information on training, including the official website of the Chartered Institute of Personnel and Development (CIPD), are included at the end of this book.

Jason De Boer is the founder and managing director of my-skills limited, establishing the company in early 2006. He has extensive business management and sales experience within the publishing sector which has included training, coaching and mentoring team members. He is a member of the Chartered Institute of Personnel and Development, and he holds the CIPD Certificate in Training Practice. Jason is also a successful business consultant, working on sales and training assignments within the publishing industry.

Introduction

This **Training Skills** book is designed to give you a concise overview of all of the core skills and tools required to be a successful trainer, based on established best practices and academic theory.

After completing this book, you will be able to –

- Distinguish between the processes of **training** and **learning**.

- Describe the **four basic stages of the learning process**.

- Use the **learning cycle** to identify different learning styles and design training which will suit each type of learner.

- Produce **professional training tools** which can be used by you or your training colleagues.

- Evaluate how well you have **delivered** a training event.

- Evaluate the **quality of learning** achieved by your participants.

- Apply tried and testing **communication skills** and **techniques for problem solving and motivating participants** during your training sessions.

Each of the first five chapters includes a set of **review questions** and **summary** notes to help you remember the skills covered, and apply them to your own training programmes. The final chapter is essentially a **toolkit** to provide practical advice and ideas for your training activities.

There is also a **Training Skills Presentation Tool** available as a Microsoft PowerPoint™ presentation show designed to support this book or to be used as a stand alone training resource.

Further details are available at **www.my-skills.co.uk**

Training Basics

What is training?
The learning cycle
Learning styles
Barriers and motivations

What is training?

This Training Skills book is designed to help you understand the key aspects of training, from the **principles** which underpin training and learning through to the **design, delivery** and **evaluation** of training courses. Whether you are a relatively inexperienced trainer looking to create or deliver a training programme, a manager looking to organize some form of training for your colleagues, or perhaps you are looking to move into training from a different field, this book will provide you with all of the essential information that you need.

Training and learning

There are many different definitions of what training actually is, but most of them agree that **training is fundamentally concerned with changing behaviour and attitudes**. Training can take many forms, from formal training programmes through to informal coaching and mentoring. This book will explore all of the methods available for delivering training.

It is also important to distinguish between training and learning, given that these two terms are often used on an interchangeable basis. **Learning** is a much broader concept which encompasses a range of processes and techniques, of which training is just one. Many people regard learning as something which happens mainly during childhood and adolescence, but it is a **constant activity** throughout our lives whether it takes place in a conscious or subconscious manner.

Stages of learning

Learning can be regarded as a cyclical process based on four key stages, and most people will move through these stages on an ongoing basis throughout their lives. **Figure TB-1** on the next page provides an overview of these learning stages.

Figure TB-1 Stages of learning

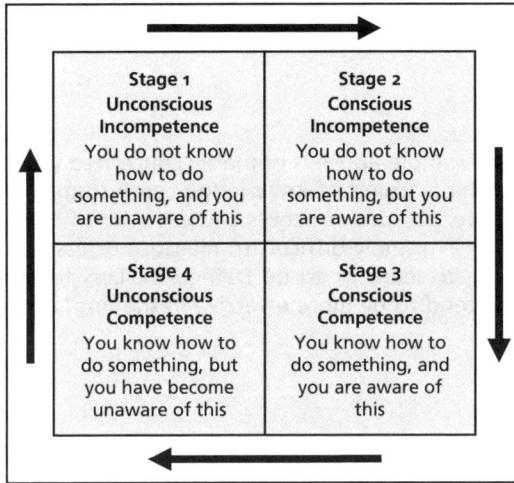

Stage 1 **Unconscious** **Incompetence** You do not know how to do something, and you are unaware of this	**Stage 2** **Conscious** **Incompetence** You do not know how to do something, but you are aware of this
Stage 4 **Unconscious** **Competence** You know how to do something, but you have become unaware of this	**Stage 3** **Conscious** **Competence** You know how to do something, and you are aware of this

For example, imagine the process of **learning to drive a car** –

- Initially this may be something about which you are unaware, perhaps due to your age (**Stage 1**), but when you get into the car for the first time you quickly become aware that you do not know how to drive and need some help (**Stage 2**).

- As your driving lessons progress, your driving competence should improve, through to the point where you take (and hopefully pass) your driving test. You are now consciously competent as a driver (**Stage 3**). You know how to drive, but you are still aware of the basic steps needed to do this, such as starting your journey by checking your mirrors, signalling and then moving away. You drive correctly, but perhaps it does not feel entirely natural.

- However, as you drive more frequently and become more confident, you will start to drive in a more natural manner without being aware of all of the steps required (**Stage 4**). It is at this stage that people can get into bad habits, forget certain steps required to drive properly, and slip back into unconscious incompetence (**Stage 1**). This is usually the point when you get a speeding ticket!

Training should be regarded as a tool for moving someone through some or all of these four stages of the learning process. The fact that someone can slip from Stage 4 (unconscious competence) back to Stage 1 (unconscious incompetence) shows that training, and learning in general, should be an ongoing process regardless of age, skills or experience.

What can be learned?

In general terms, learning (and therefore training) covers three core aspects –

- Attitudes
- Skills
- Knowledge

The driving lesson example above is primarily concerned with the learning of and training in **skills**. The learning of **knowledge** can include basic facts and figures through to far more detailed concepts such as scientific or technical processes. **Attitudes** are often extremely difficult to measure or assess, and as such are the most difficult thing to learn or to be trained in. Less formal learning methods such as mentoring tend to be more effective in shaping attitudes, and as a result changing behaviour.

The learning cycle

The theme of learning as an ongoing and constant process can also be applied to the process of learning a **specific** attitude, skill or knowledge, and by extension to the process of undertaking training in each of these aspects.

Over the last three decades writers such as **Kolb** (1974) and **Honey & Mumford** (1992) have developed the idea of the **learning cycle**. This fundamental concept is summarized in **Figure TB-2** below.

Figure TB-2 The learning cycle

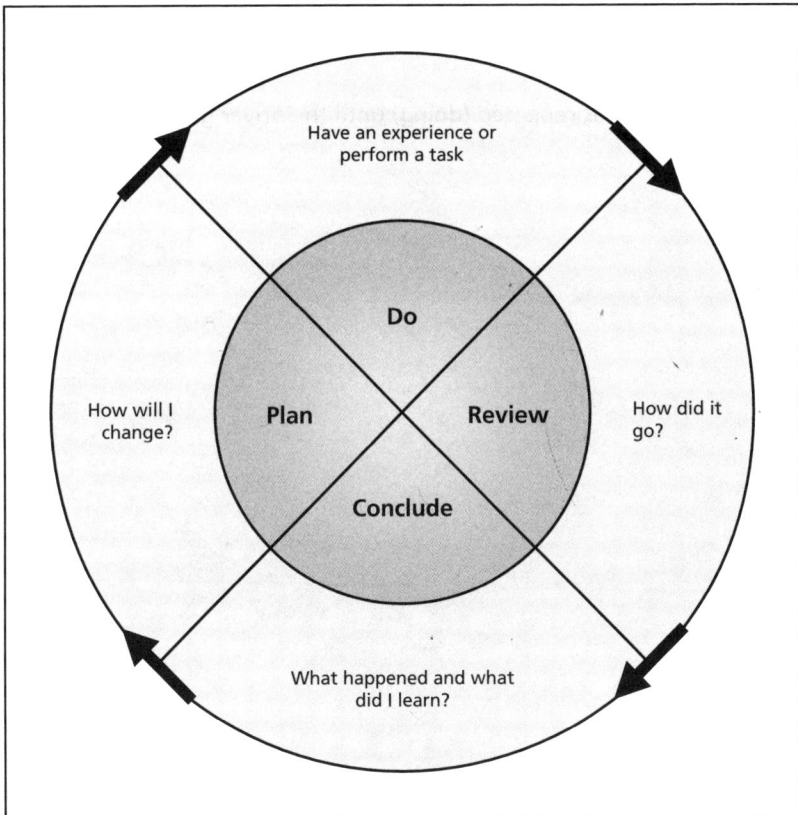

Different people learn in different ways, and this is covered in the next section. However, if learning and training are to be effective, each of the steps in the learning cycle **must** be covered.

It is worth referring back to the previous example of a driving lesson in order to provide a simple illustration.

- For instance, the driver attempts to reverse park between two cars (the **doing** part of the learning cycle), but finds it difficult to control the speed of the car and handle the reverse turn at the same time (**reviewing**).

- As a result, the car hits the pavement or the stationery car parked behind, because the driver could not handle the car at that particular speed (**concluding**).

- The driver decides that he/she needs to slow down and concentrate fully on steering the car into the space without touching the kerb or any of the parked cars (**planning**).

- The manoeuvre is repeated (**doing**) until the driver gets it right.

Learning styles

The learning cycle discussed in the previous section is particularly relevant to **adult learners**, and as a trainer it is important to recognize the differences between adult learning and childhood learning commonly associated with school classes.

Experiential learning

Many people are put off by the idea of attending a training course. They are often 'sent' on a course by a manager or supervisor, and regard it as a return to the classroom. There are some good reasons for this reaction. The main difference between adults and children is **experience**, whether it is experience of life, study or work. Experience is at the centre of adult learning, and as a trainer it is important to plan and deliver training that builds upon the experiences of the learner. On the other side of the coin, these experiences may have created **preconceptions** and attitudes which can impact upon an individual's ability to learn. Again, the trainer needs to develop a training programme which will explore and if necessary counter these preconceptions.

The best way to use the experiences of a group of learners, and to address any misgivings or preconceptions within the group, is to use training methods which make direct use of the following techniques –

- Group discussions

- Problem solving activities

- Project work

- Simulation or roleplay exercises

These methods allow learners to share experiences and challenge each others' assumptions. The role of the trainer is to facilitate this process within a safe and supportive environment, and ensure that it moves the group towards meeting their learning objectives. These factors are covered in more detail in the **Designing & Delivering Training** chapter.

Different approaches to learning

Although learning can be defined as a coherent process by using a tool such as the learning cycle, it is vital to recognize that different people tend to learn in different ways, and as a result will respond to different training methods in different ways. There are a range of different models that have been developed to categorize individual approaches to learning, but the two most commonly used are –

- The four learning styles (**Honey & Mumford**)
- The eight multiple intelligences (**Gardner**)

Both of these models are relatively straightforward, and are explained in more detail on the following pages.

The four learning styles model

This is the most commonly used learning model, given that it relates directly to the learning cycle. Each part of the cycle lends itself to a certain style of learning, and this is illustrated in **Figure TB-3** below.

Figure TB-3 The four learning styles model

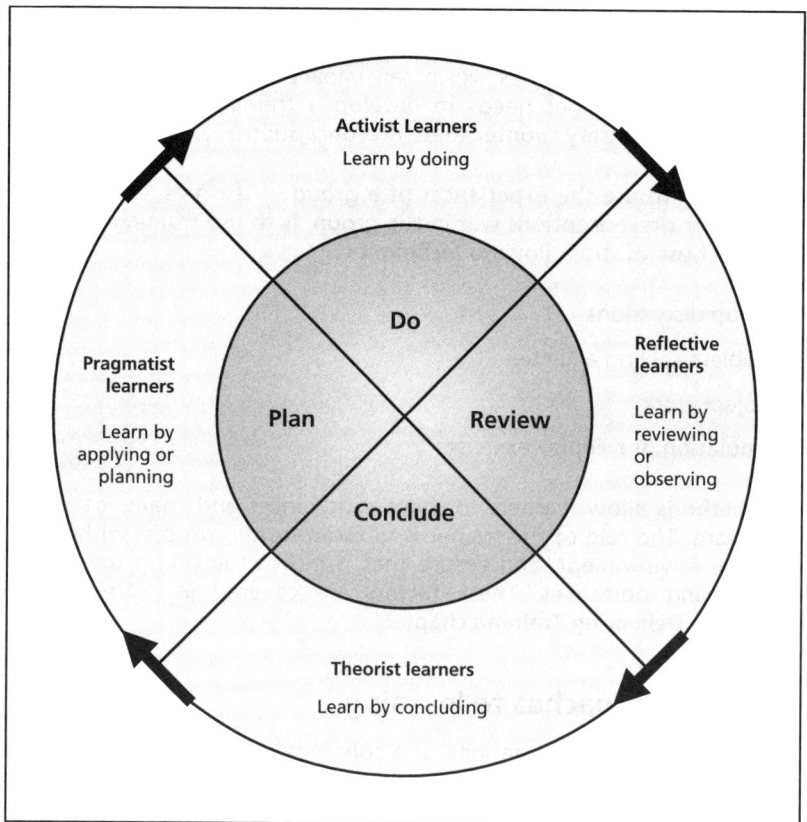

Within this model, different types of learner respond to different types of learning activities. For example –

Table TB-1 Preferred learning methods for each learning style

	Prefer to learn by	Tend not to enjoy learning by
Activists	✓ Problem solving ✓ Experimenting ✓ Brainstorming ✓ Competitive exercises ✓ Group discussion ✓ Roleplay or simulation	✗ Observation ✗ Repetition ✗ Analyzing data ✗ Creating or discussing theories
Reflectors	✓ Reviewing previous experiences ✓ Observation ✓ Discussing pros and cons ✓ Planning activities	✗ Roleplay or simulation ✗ Being placed on the spot by the trainer or colleagues
Theorists	✓ Reading handouts with large amounts of theory and information ✓ Applying a theory to a situation ✓ Analyzing data ✓ Problems with clear outcomes	✗ Being placed in emotive situations ✗ Activities or exercises without a clearly defined outcome or goal
Pragmatists	✓ Practical activities and exercises ✓ Creating action plans ✓ Relating the learning to their own job or situation	✗ Theory based sessions ✗ Being given concepts without application to real situations

It is impossible and impractical to pigeon-hole every individual learner within these categories, but they do provide a useful guide when planning and delivering a training session.

The eight multiple intelligences model

This model is based on eight core characteristics or **intelligences** which contribute to an individual's ability to create things or solve problems. A person can possess some or all of these characteristics, which are summarized below.

Table TB-2 Preferred learning methods for each intelligence

	Prefer to learn by
Linguistic	✓ Reading and writing ✓ Listening to a speaker or an audio source
Mathematical or Logical	✓ Solving problems and puzzles ✓ Finding patterns and trends
Visual or Spatial	✓ Observation ✓ Looking at illustrations and diagrams ✓ Watching DVDs and videos
Musical	✓ Listening to sounds and music
Interpersonal	✓ Hearing other people's views and experiences ✓ Teamwork activities
Intrapersonal	✓ Working independently ✓ Reflecting on their own experiences
Physical	✓ Physical activities and tasks ✓ Practical exercises
Naturalist	✓ Working in the open air ✓ Studying their environment

Again, these categories can be a useful aid when preparing and running a training programme.

It can be difficult to determine how each learner within your group compares with these learning models during a training session, but they can provide a framework for your preparation, and this is covered in further detail in the **Designing & Delivering Training** chapter.

Barriers and motivations

As a trainer it is important to understand why people sometimes struggle to learn, and what kind of factors encourage people to learn. These **barriers** and **motivations** should have an influence on how you prepare, design and deliver a training programme. One useful way to approach this is to consider **internal** and **external** factors in each case.

Barriers to learning

Internal barriers to learning can include some or all of the following –

- **Negative experiences** in the past, such as performing badly at school or on previous training courses, or failing to meet the learning objectives for a previous course.

- **Poor achievement** prior to the training programme, perhaps in basic skill areas such as literacy, numeracy or information technology.

- **Insufficient aptitude** for a particular activity or course, such as a physical impairment or learning difficulty.

- A **lack of motivation** on the part of the learner, which may be due to any of the factors above, or to the scenario suggested earlier in this chapter of a learner being 'sent' on a training course by their manager with minimal discussion or consent.

External barriers are more readily apparent, and the trainer is often in a position to address these directly before or during a training session –

- The **training environment**, which may include factors such as the room layout, noise and climate.

- **Other learners** participating in the training, some of whom may tend to dominate the session due to their personality or may simply be disruptive.

- The **trainer** could be a barrier to learning, due to poor preparation, poor delivery or poor interaction with members of the group. This book should help you to avoid this barrier!

The chapter on **Designing & Delivering Training** discusses ways in which a trainer can address each of these potential barriers to learning.

Motivations to learning

A large amount of research has been conducted into the theory of motivation, from **Maslow's hierarchy of needs** (1943), which views motivation as a series of ascending steps from food and shelter up to personal fulfilment, through to the idea of **rewards as motivation** first put forward by **Otto & Glaser** (1970). This is a useful model for identifying **internal** motivations, and can be summarized as follows –

- Personal **achievement** or success

- Avoiding **failure** or ridicule

- Gaining **approval** or recognition from peers or managers

- Satisfying **curiosity**

This model also includes a set of **external** motivations, namely –

- Acquiring **physical** or **tangible** rewards such as money, promotion or gifts.

All of these motivational factors point towards one of the most common and important questions asked by people who are about to undertake a training programme – **what's in it for me?** If you can address this basic question before, during and after your training session, you will go a long way to ensuring a successful outcome for everyone involved.

Review questions

Bearing in mind your own experiences in planning and delivering training, or perhaps referring to a training session in which you have been recently involved, consider how you would answer the following questions.

1   What are the four basic stages of learning?

2   Can you give a recent example of a situation in which you have moved through each stage of this process?

3   Based on the four learning styles and the eight multiple intelligences, what kind of learner would you consider yourself to be?

4   What types of barriers to learning have you encountered in recent training events, either from your own perspective or that of your training group?

5   How did you deal with these barriers, and what would you do differently in the future?

Summary

- Training is fundamentally concerned with **changing behaviour and attitudes**.

- Training is just one of a number of techniques for **learning**.

- There are **four basic stages of the learning process** – unconscious incompetence, conscious incompetence, conscious competence and unconscious competence. This is a cyclical process.

- Learning and training cover three core aspects – **attitudes**, **skills** and **knowledge**.

- The learning process can be described in four steps known as the **learning cycle – do, review, conclude** and **plan**.

- The best method for adult learning is **experiential learning**.

- Different types of learner respond to different training methods.

- The most important question for a trainer to address is – **what's in it for me?**

Learning Needs Analysis

What is a learning need?
Levels of learning need
The importance of business needs
Personal learning needs

What is a learning need?

Before a programme of learning or training can be started, it is often necessary to establish the reasons **why** the training is required. If you are an external training consultant brought in to an organization to deliver a programme, this process may well have already been undertaken by the organization itself. However, if you are a trainer within an organization being asked to recommend training programmes, or if you are a business manager trying to address performance issues within your team, you will need to establish the **learning needs** of the team or individuals concerned.

In basic terms, a learning need is a **gap** or shortfall between the current situation and the required or desired situation. For example, a sales team may be underperforming against their revenue targets or profitability goals. Part of the sales manager's job will be to establish why this underperformance has occurred, and what can be done to address it. The sales manager may decide to involve a training consultant or HR colleague in this process.

This example is also helpful in illustrating whether a particular gap or shortfall is due to a learning need or another problem. If the sales team is underperforming despite having all of the capabilities and tools required to achieve its given goals, then this is essentially a management problem, which admittedly may involve an element of training in dealing with it. If the sales team is simply unable to achieve its given goals due to a lack of capability rather than effort, then the problem is essentially one of learning.

Factors which suggest or create learning needs

As a trainer or manager you should be aware of certain factors which could indicate learning needs on the part of individuals, teams or a whole organization. These factors may include –

- Declining performance against specific targets or goals
- Declining market share or performance against direct competitors
- Declining productivity
- Deterioration in staff behaviour and morale
- Increasing disputes
- Increasing customer complaints and dissatisfaction
- Increasing number of accidents
- Increasing wastage
- Increasing turnover of staff

- New government legislation
- New industry standards
- New technology or systems within the organization
- New plant and machinery
- New products
- New jobs or additional responsibilities

How to identify a learning need

It is important to distinguish between **needs** and **wants**. For instance, when asked about their development needs, a sales person may ask for extensive training on a particular product, but from a business management perspective this may be of relatively limited benefit when compared to developing the account management or closing skills of the same sales person.

One way to identify a **real** learning need is to ask yourself the following three simple questions –

- Is it **relevant** to the role of the individual or team?
- Is the person or group **capable** of learning this particular need?
- Are they **motivated** to learn it?

If you can answer yes to all three questions, the learning need is genuine and should be pursued further. This is also a useful way of **prioritizing** learning needs.

Levels of learning need

The list of factors contributing to learning needs in the previous section covers a range of levels which can be categorized as follows –

- **Organizational** learning needs which apply to a whole business or institution.

- **Group** or occupational learning needs which apply to a team or specific job role.

- **Individual** or personal learning needs which apply to a single employee or team member.

Training has traditionally been used as a corrective measure to address underperformance or shortcomings on the part of individuals within an organization, and the impetus for identifying training needs generally comes from line managers or supervisors who are responsible for the overall performance of their team. This is a very narrow view of the training process, and ignores many of the wider benefits that training and learning in general can provide. **Boydell & Leary** (1996) have created a useful grid (**Figure LN-1**) which allows a trainer to identify learning needs in terms of the level of **need** and the level of **benefit**.

Figure LN-1 Levels of learning need and benefit

Level of need Level of benefit	Organizational	Group	Individual
Implementing Doing things well	Meeting current organizational objectives	Working together to meet existing targets and standards	Being competent at the level of existing requirements
Improving Doing things better	Setting higher objectives and reaching them	Continuous improvement teams	Having and using systematic, continuous improvement skills and processes
Innovating Doing new and better things	Changing objectives and strategies	Working across boundaries to create new relationships and new products and services	Being able to work differently and more creatively with a shared sense of purpose

The traditional view of training fits into the **individual/implementing** level of learning need, i.e. correcting shortfalls by getting individuals up to existing standards of competence or performance. For training to be really effective in improving individuals, groups and organizations, it is worth taking a broader and longer term view as suggested by this grid.

This takes us on to the next section, which looks at type of factors that should be the driving force behind learning and training.

The importance of business needs

A central tenet of learning needs analysis is the importance of the overall needs of the **organization** or **business (Bee & Bee** 2003). Whatever someone's role may be within an organization, from its head to a team member, they will ultimately be working to achieve the stated goals of that organization, whether they are based on financial considerations, undertaking specific activities or on ethical dimensions.

This emphasis on business needs places the **business plan** of the organization at the heart of learning needs analysis, as opposed to ad hoc requests from line managers or individuals within the organization.

Business needs can be created by the need to **grow, consolidate, contract** or in some instances **close.** For example, if a business aims to sell new products or move into new markets, there is likely to be a need to develop its staff across a range of departments, from sales and marketing through to production and operations. At the other end of the spectrum, if a business is faced with closure there may be an ethical or social need to provide staff with training opportunities in new areas. The recent collapse of the MG Rover car manufacturing business in the West Midlands is a recent example of this, where staff have been offered training in new areas such as information technology skills.

There may also be external factors which impact upon business needs. These can include customer behaviour, increased competition, technological changes, demographic changes, economic factors and political changes.

Business needs, and the specific training needs which arise, form the first two stages of the **learning and development cycle** illustrated on the next page in **Figure LN-2.** This is a more detailed version of the learning cycle described in the previous chapter, using the same cyclical model to describe a process of continuous improvement.

The next chapter of this book provides practical advice for covering the third and fourth stages of the learning and development cycle.

Figure LN-2 The learning and development cycle (training cycle)

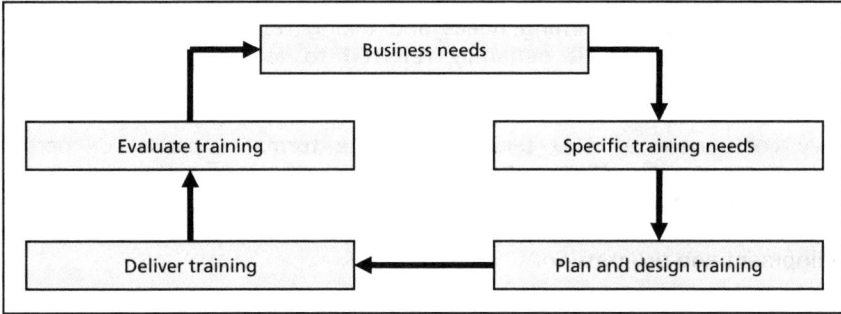

Personal learning needs

Many organizations now place a strong emphasis on employees or members identifying their own learning needs and taking responsibility for their own learning activities. This is generally referred to as **continuing professional development** (CPD).

A key component of CPD tends to be the formal appraisal or personal development plan, especially within a corporate environment. However, this can often be driven purely by business requirements and if done badly can become an assessment process rather than a two-way conversation regarding development and progression.

There are some simple tools available which can help you to plan and manage your own CPD. This is of particular importance if you are a member of a professional body.

The easiest method is to conduct a **personal SWOT analysis**, identifying your own strengths, weaknesses, opportunities and threats. **Table LN-1** below provides a simple illustration of a SWOT analysis template.

Table LN-1 Simple illustration of a personal SWOT analysis template

Internal	Strengths	Weaknesses
	Summary:	Summary:
	Skills:	Skills:
	Experience:	Experience:
	Attitude:	Attitude:
External	Opportunities	Threats
	Industry or Sector:	Industry or Sector:
	Technology:	Technology:
	Policies or Legislation:	Policies or Legislation:
	Other:	Other:

Review questions

Bearing in mind your own experiences in planning and delivering training, or perhaps referring to a training session in which you have been recently involved, consider how you would answer the following questions.

1   What is a learning need?

2   What specific learning need indicators have you encountered in a recent work or training situation?

3   At what level did each of these learning needs occur (organizational, group or individual)?

4   How important are the needs of your business or organization at the moment in terms of identifying learning needs and specifying training events?

5   What can you do to address this within your organization, and who else would need to be involved?

Summary

- A learning need is a **gap** or shortfall between the current situation and the required or desired situation.

- There are three factors which can determine whether something is a learning need or a want – **relevance, capability** and **motivation** on the part of the learner.

- There are three levels at which learning needs occur – **organizational, group** and **individual.**

- **Business needs** are central to learning needs analysis.

- A personal SWOT analysis is an effective way to manage your own **continuing professional development.**

Designing & Delivering Training

Learning objectives
Training methods
Tools for the trainer
In the training room

Learning objectives

Earlier in this book, the process of training was defined as being concerned with the act of changing behaviour and attitudes. In order to determine how effective a training programme has been, you need to be able to provide some kind of **measurement**. This is where **learning objectives** are absolutely vital.

Writing good learning objectives

Every good training programme is based on a set of learning objectives, whether it is a classroom based session, a work based activity or a text based study tool such as this book. There are four key points which must be taken into account whenever you write a learning objective –

- Learning objectives should be based on **observable behaviours** or **observable changes in attitude**. This means that the wording used must be very specific and clear.

- It is important to distinguish between **aims** and objectives. Aims can be quite general and include words such as **understand, know** and **appreciate**. However, objectives need to be very specific, which means that these general words should be avoided whenever possible, however tempting it may be to use them!

- A learning objective should refer to a **single** change in behaviour or attitude, and you should avoid including multiple objectives in one statement.

- Each learning objective should be **relevant** to the needs of the learner in terms of its intention and scope.

Table DT-1 below illustrates some examples of good and bad action verbs for writing learning objectives.

Table DT-1 Good and bad action verbs for learning objectives

Good				Bad	
✓	Apply	✓	Describe	✗	Appreciate
✓	Appraise	✓	Evaluate	✗	Believe
✓	Compare	✓	Identify	✗	Feel
✓	Conduct	✓	Outline	✗	Know
✓	Contrast	✓	Predict	✗	Understand
✓	Criticise	✓	Prepare		
✓	Define	✓	Specify		
✓	Demonstrate	✓	State		

SMART learning objectives

It can also be useful to apply the tried and tested **SMART** principle to your learning objectives, in other words making each one –

- Specific

- Measurable

- Achievable

- Realistic (or result oriented)

- Time based

Applying all of these criteria, one example of a learning objective could be –

- After reading the first chapter of the Training Skills book, you will be able to identify four different styles of learner within your study group.

This objective is very **specific** (it refers to the single objective of identifying the four learning styles), **measurable** (you will either be able to identify all four styles, some of them or none of them), **achievable** and **realistic** (it is a relatively small aspect of the training process), and **time based** (you should be able to do it after reading the first chapter). It also relates directly to a **relevant** situation (working with a study group).

Training methods

Before you can decide **how** you are going to design and deliver a training programme, you need to ask two other questions – **why** and **who**? This involves looking at two specific areas before you decide upon the most appropriate training method –

- The purpose of the training

- The profile of the learners

Much of this has been covered in previous chapters, but the key points are summarized below with some additional ideas.

The purpose of the training

The purpose of the training is driven by the **learning needs** identified by the trainer or manager. As discussed earlier, these learning needs may be relevant to individual learners, groups of learners or the organization as a whole. Is there one specific learning need, or a series of learning needs that are required to achieve a specific goal? For example, does a sales person need training on a specific product, or do they require a full course of sales training as part of an overall induction programme? The former learning need may be met through coaching from a product specialist, whereas the latter may require a structured classroom based training programme followed by ongoing mentoring from a line manager.

The next step is to determine the type of learning that is required. Is it based primarily on the development of **skills, knowledge, attitudes** or a combination of all three? Another way of looking at this is to use the **CRAMP** framework –

- **Comprehension**
  Developing a general understanding of a topic

- **Reflex**
  Developing physical or mental responses

- **Attitude**
  Developing or changing attitudes

- **Memory**
  Developing the ability to recall information and data

- **Procedures**
  Developing familiarity with important or mandatory procedures and methods

It is also worth remembering the basic **stages of learning** covered at the start of this book. Is the purpose of the training to move someone from unconscious incompetence to conscious competence (e.g. learning something for the first time), or to return someone to competence after slipping into a state of unconscious incompetence (e.g. developing best practices to counteract growing inefficiency)? This may also have a bearing on the training methods selected.

The profile of the learners

Once the purpose of the training has been established, you need to consider the profile of the learners when designing your training programme.

It is easy to generalize or to adopt a 'one size fits all' approach to training, especially if the programme is for a large group of learners or if it has been run previously with an established set of learning materials and training notes. There are two ways in which you can avoid these pitfalls, depending on your relationship with the learners and the time available before and during the training programme itself.

If possible, conduct some **research** before the training event to gain an insight into the preferred learning styles or characteristics of the study group. If you are a manager or in-house trainer you may already have a good idea of the learning preferences of individual learners. However, if you are an external consultant it may be a good idea to ask each participant to complete a **preliminary questionnaire** a few days before the training event. This questionnaire can include some multiple choice questions designed to provide an overview of each participants' learning preferences. It can also be used to assess current levels of knowledge, skills or attitudes, in order to help the trainer to design the programme with the appropriate level of scope and range of content.

However, it is not always feasible to conduct this kind of advance research before delivering an event. In this case, it is important to make the training programme as **varied** as possible in order to appeal to as many learning styles as you can, and to try to keep all of the learners involved throughout the session.

When designing a training programme it is also vital to take into account any relevant **diversity** and **disability** issues. Certain topics or training methods may have implications for certain religious or ethnic groups. For example, prolonged direct eye contact from a trainer to a learner may be frowned upon by certain groups, or perhaps certain discussion topics may prove offensive for certain people. Learners with visual impairments may struggle to read handouts and presentation slides, whilst students with impaired hearing may have difficulty in following comments from the trainer or other group members. Learners with physical disabilities may have a problem with exercises and group work which involve extensive movement or exertion.

Advance research is helpful in making the trainer aware of these issues, but it is also worth addressing them discreetly at the start of a training programme. This is a practical approach which also demonstrates a good level of consideration on the part of the trainer towards group members.

Selecting training methods

At this stage you should be ready to plan **how** you are going to deliver the required training. **Table DT-2** below provides an overview of the benefits and potential drawbacks of each training method, and shows how each method can address the purpose of the training and the profile of the learners. Some advice on preparing each of these methods follows the overview.

Table DT-2 Selecting training methods

Method	Benefits	Drawbacks	Purpose	Profile
Lectures, talks and presentations	Good for large groups of learners Good for presenting large amounts of information	Low level of feedback Hard to assess level of learning Learners are passive Can be inappropriate for learners with hearing or visual disabilities	Sharing knowledge Developing comprehension	Reflectors Theorists Linguistic Interpersonal Intrapersonal Visual
Discussion groups	Maximizes experiences within the group Involves all members of the group Reinforces understanding of a topic	Some people may participate more than others and dominate the discussion Difficult to control Time consuming	Sharing knowledge Developing skills Shaping attitudes Developing comprehension	Activists Reflectors Interpersonal
Brainstorming activities	Supports participation by all learners Builds on group experiences Helps creative thinking	Time consuming Heavily dependent on good facilitation by the trainer Often unfocused	Sharing knowledge	Activists Pragmatists Interpersonal Logical

Table DT-2 Selecting training methods (continued)

Method	Benefits	Drawbacks	Purpose	Profile
Roleplay and simulation activities	Gives learners an opportunity to practice skills Opportunity to observe others Encourages empathy between learners	Can be intimidating if conducted with a large audience Difficult for the trainer to observe or facilitate all roleplays in a large group	Developing skills Shaping attitudes	Activists Pragmatists Visual Interpersonal Physical
DVDs and videos	Encourages discussion Encourages reflection Reinforces points covered in a lecture or presentation Can look professional Provides a natural break in a long session	Needs to be placed in context by the trainer Can lead to distractions May be inappropriate for learners with visual or hearing disabilities	Sharing knowledge Developing skills Shaping attitudes	Reflectors Pragmatists Visual Musical Interpersonal Intrapersonal
Practical exercises or tests	Allow learners to develop skills through practice and repetition	May require close supervision from the trainer Time consuming May require specialist tools or machinery	Developing skills Developing reflexes Learning procedures Developing comprehension Assessing competence Improving memory	Pragmatists Activists Physical
Self study and e-learning	Learner driven so generally not time constrained Allows self paced learning Low cost	Possible lack of trainer or group support Difficult to observe	Building knowledge Developing skills	Theorists Activists Linguistic Visual Intrapersonal

Lectures, talks and presentations

Benefits

- Good for large groups of learners
- Good for presenting large amounts of information

Drawbacks

- Low level of feedback
- Hard to assess the level of learning
- Learners are passive
- Can be inappropriate for learners with hearing or visual disabilities

Purpose

- Sharing knowledge
- Developing comprehension

Profile

- Reflectors
- Theorists
- Linguistic
- Interpersonal
- Intrapersonal
- Visual

Preparation

All of these should be properly structured and timed, with a clear introduction and summary. Visual aids and handouts should be relevant and complementary rather than distracting. Theory and knowledge should be balanced with examples and relevant anecdotes.

If you are preparing Microsoft PowerPoint™ slides use a simple clear design, a large font size with plenty of space between lines, and try to limit the text on each slide to a maximum of six bullet points. Any more than this and the audience will be concentrating on the slide show to the detriment of your comments. Keep slide animations straightforward as well – simple fades are usually the most professional looking and least distracting.

Discussion groups

Benefits

- Maximizes experiences within the group
- Involves all members of the group
- Reinforces understanding of a topic

Drawbacks

- Some people may participate more than others and dominate the discussion
- Difficult to control
- Time consuming

Purpose

- Sharing knowledge
- Developing skills
- Shaping attitudes
- Developing comprehension

Profile

- Activists
- Reflectors
- Interpersonal

Preparation

Planning and facilitation are essential for focused discussions which move learners towards their learning objectives. Having clear timings and asking each group to report back to the rest of the learners with specific conclusions and comments can help in this regard.

Brainstorming activities

Benefits

- Supports participation by all learners in the group
- Builds on group experiences
- Helps creative thinking

Drawbacks

- Time consuming
- Heavily dependent on good facilitation by the trainer
- Often unfocused

Purpose

- Sharing knowledge

Profile

- Activists
- Pragmatists
- Interpersonal
- Logical

Preparation

This should require minimal planning on the part of the trainer, except for choosing an appropriate topic and having some ideas of his/her own to stimulate debate if the group struggles initially. Flipcharts, whiteboards or adhesive note pads are the best ways to collate ideas. The latter are especially good for structured brainstorming techniques such as mind mapping, the Concept Fan or brain writing, enabling ideas to be moved and placed in a specific order after the initial brainstorming activity. These techniques are discussed in detail later in this book.

Roleplay and simulation activities

Benefits

- Gives learners an opportunity to practice skills
- Provides an opportunity to observe others
- Encourages empathy between learners

Drawbacks

- Can be intimidating if conducted in front of a large audience
- Difficult for the trainer to observe or facilitate all roleplays in a large group

Purpose

- Developing skills

- Shaping attitudes

Profile

- Reflectors

- Pragmatists

- Visual

- Musical

- Interpersonal

- Intrapersonal

Preparation

There are two crucial aspects to a successful roleplay or simulation – detailed preparation of the scenario, and the creation of a completely safe environment for the participants. Without clearly defined roles and objectives for the roleplay, participants may find it difficult to successfully complete their respective parts.

Asking participants to perform a roleplay in front of a large audience or whilst being recorded on video should be avoided. The point of the exercise is to experience the respective roles within a situation and practice specific skills, not to have a performance judged by the trainer or fellow learners. The best arrangement for a roleplay is to have two or three participants and one or two observers, all of whom are learners within the same group. Each learner should take it in turn to adopt each role and to observe their colleagues.

DVDs and videos

Benefits

- Encourages discussion amongst learners

- Encourages reflection by learners

- Reinforces points covered in a lecture or presentation

- Can look professional

- Provides a natural break in a long session

Drawbacks

- Needs to be placed in context by the trainer

- Can lead to distractions

- May be inappropriate for learners with visual or hearing disabilities

Purpose

- Sharing knowledge
- Developing skills
- Shaping attitudes

Profile

- Reflectors
- Pragmatists
- Visual
- Musical
- Interpersonal
- Intrapersonal

Preparation

The main concern here should be technical preparation. It is a good idea to check all audio/visual equipment before the start of a training session, whether it is a traditional video player, a multimedia suite or an audio/video clip embedded in a Microsoft PowerPoint™ presentation. If you are using a USB memory stick to deliver a presentation from a third party PC or laptop, ensure that any audio/video clips are saved separately on the same memory stick along with the presentation itself. You should also be prepared for any unforeseen technical problems, and have contingency measures in place such as handouts or alternative activities.

Practical exercises or tests

Benefits

- Allows learners to develop skills through practice and repetition

Drawbacks

- May require close supervision from the trainer
- Time consuming
- May require specialist tools or machinery

Purpose

- Developing skills
- Developing reflexes

- Learning procedures
- Developing comprehension
- Assessing competence
- Improving memory

Profile

- Pragmatists
- Activists
- Physical

Preparation

Describing this kind of activity as an exercise rather than a test may help to reduce any sense of apprehension on the part of your participants. Sometimes these activities can be used before a training event as a diagnostic tool, to help potential participants, line managers and trainers to identify specific learning needs and to determine who within the organization would benefit the most from being involved in a related training session.

Self study and e-learning

Benefits

- Learner driven so generally not time constrained
- Allows self paced learning
- Relatively low cost compared to a formal classroom based training event

Drawbacks

- Possible lack of trainer or group support
- Difficult for a trainer to observe

Purpose

- Building knowledge
- Developing skills

Profile

- Theorists
- Activists
- Linguistic

- Visual

- Intrapersonal

Preparation

Self study materials and activities can be used to supplement formal training sessions in order to reinforce learning or to reduce costs for the organization. Alternatively, self study can be a substitute for formal training, especially for personal self development as part of a continuing professional development (CPD) programme. For individual learners, the majority of their preparation will focus on time management and finding the right learning materials for their needs.

Tools for trainers

Whilst a great deal of emphasis is placed on materials and tools for learners, such as presentation slides, handouts and audio/visual resources, one area often neglected is that of **tools for trainers** themselves. This is of particular importance when a group of trainers are delivering the same training programme to **different groups**, such as call centre training across multiple sites, or when a training programme is likely to be **repeated on a regular basis**, such as induction training for new hires or basic sales skills training.

Most trainers will have a set of notes to help them during the session, but there are two structured documents that can be of great benefit when preparing training programmes for multiple or repeat delivery –

- Session plan

- Tutor notes

These documents help to provide a **consistent** approach to delivering a training session, and each is discussed in detail below.

Session plan

The session plan is designed to help a trainer to stay in control of the **overall structure** of a training session in terms of timings and resources. It also helps the trainer to remain focused on the specific learning objectives for the session, and to understand how each objective fits into each part of the session. The plan can be produced in a range of formats, but ideally it should be on one or two pages so that it can be viewed easily by the trainer during a session, it should be structured in terms of presentation slide progression and/or specific learning outcomes, and it should include the following key information –

- **Timings** in terms of minutes elapsed, and if appropriate **presentation slide numbers**.

- Details of the required **learning outcomes** for each part of the session.

- The **training method** to be used for that part of the session, such as directed training (lecture or presentation slides), group activity, roleplay, brainstorming or individual activity.

- A summary of the **key points** to be made or discussed within that part of the session.

- The **resources** required during that part of the session, such as presentation slides, audio/visual material, flipcharts or handouts. Reference numbers for each resource are also useful.

This kind of plan also helps a trainer to deliver a session which is based on a mix of training methods, and to manage this mix efficiently. **Figure DT-1** on the next page provides a simple illustration of the format for a session plan.

Figure DT-1 Outline format for a training session plan

Time	Learning outcomes	Training method	Points to be made or discussed	Resources
00:00 to 05:00 minutes Slides 1 - 3	What is the aim of this part of the session? How does it relate to the learning objectives?	For example – DT Directed Training GA Group Activity RP Roleplay BS Brainstorm IA Individual Activity HO Handout QA Question & Answer	What do you as trainer plan to say and do during this part of the session? Are there any specific points of activities that you need to remember?	A referenced list of all required resources for this part of the session, such as presentation slides, handouts, audio/visual aids, flipcharts or activity materials

Tutor notes

Tutor notes (sometimes referred to as **facilitator notes**) are closer to the traditional type of notes which a lecturer or presenter may use during whilst delivering a session. These notes provide **detailed information** for each part of the training session, and are often in the form of a script with detailed comments and prompts. Given that most formal training sessions use Microsoft PowerPoint™ presentation slides as the main method of delivery, the easiest method is to use the notes facility within this software application to create detailed tutor notes. This provides a natural structure for the notes based on a single page of information for each presentation slide.

It makes sense for the tutor notes to use a similar timing structure to the session plan for consistency and ease of understanding. Each page of the tutor notes should have a header which includes a title (often the title of the presentation slide), the slide or section number (for example, Slide 1) and an approximate timing (for example, 00:00 to 02:00 minutes).

Using bullet points will make the script easy to read and follow during a session, and it is helpful to have prompts, directions or supplementary comments in a different font, different colour and/or italicized. As a competent trainer you are unlikely to read the script verbatim whilst delivering a training session, but it is reassuring to have the script available just in case you lose track for a moment. It is also extremely useful for a new or inexperienced trainer who is given an existing training session to deliver at short notice.

In the training room

Once all of the preparation for the training session is complete, it is important to remember a few useful tips that will help you to stay in control on the day, involve all of the learners, and help everyone to enjoy the session (including you).

- **Arrive early**, at least twenty minutes before the first participants start to arrive. This will give you an opportunity to check the room layout and any equipment that will be used during the session.

- Try to **personally greet** each of the learners, ideally over a coffee before the session begins. It will make your formal introduction to the session easier, and it will make each of the learners feel that they have a degree of involvement with the session and with you as the trainer right from the outset. It also provides a window for any latecomers to arrive.

- There are few things more disconcerting for a group of learners than being sat in a room waiting for the session to begin, and then the trainer walks in unannounced and starts the formal training. It harks back to the school classroom, and may create an unhelpful feeling of subordination on the part of the learners. There are **no subordinates** within a training room.

- Make sure that the **training environment** is appropriate for your training session and for the participants. If you are planning to run a programme based on group activities, a lecture theatre style seating arrangement is unlikely to yield the best results. Try to control factors such as noise and climate before the participants arrive (check the air conditioning and windows), and ensure that there are sufficient provisions for learners with sensory or physical disabilities.

- **Housekeeping** is important. Let the group know when breaks will occur, and where they can locate facilities such as toilets and drinking water. Ask the participants to switch their mobile phones, Blackberry™ devices and PDAs to silent, but provide them with enough time during breaks to check their messages and make any important calls. The last thing you want as a trainer is for people to be e-mailing and texting colleagues, customers or even fellow participants across the room! Try to schedule a break every 60-90 minutes.

- Remember the first and most fundamental question that a learner will ask themselves at the start of a training session – **what's in it for me?** If you can address this during your introduction, it will go a long way to creating a positive mood within the group and helping the session to go smoothly. For example, if you are delivering financial skills training to non-financial staff, try to relate it to their own roles and experiences through examples, anecdotes and questioning.

- If you have addressed all of these points, you are more than half way towards having a good training session. However, if you are a nervous speaker or new to training, you may still have problems with nerves at the start of the session. Remember to breathe (not as stupid as it sounds!), talk slowly, engage with the participants through smiling, eye contact and (if appropriate) a joke, and use the available floor space to move around the room. If you are really nervous, start the training with an icebreaker or a video clip to divert attention away from you.

Review questions

Bearing in mind your own experiences in planning and delivering training, or perhaps referring to a training session in which you have been recently involved, consider how you would answer the following questions.

1   What are the main principles involved in writing good learning objectives?

2   What criteria would you use for selecting a set of training methods for a particular training event?

3   When would you use a roleplay activity with your participants?

4   Have you used a formal session plan in your recent training events? What key information would you include in future session plans?

5   Name three things which you can address on the day and should help you to run a successful training session.

Summary

- In order to determine how effective a training programme has been, you need some kind of **measurement**. This is best achieved through **learning objectives**.

- Learning objectives should be based on **observable** behaviours or changes in attitude. The wording used must be very specific and clear, and the objective should refer to a **single** change.

- The selection of training methods should be based on two factors – the **purpose** of the learning, and the **profile** of the learners.

- Developing professional training tools such as a **session plan** and **tutor notes** will help you and your colleagues to deliver the same training event to different groups across multiple sites, or to manage a regularly repeated training programme.

- Remember the **basic tips** for running a training event on the day – this will help you to stay in control, involve all of the learners, and help everyone to enjoy the session.

Evaluation & Assessment

What is evaluation?
Evaluation tools
Questionnaires

What is evaluation?

If training is designed to change behaviour and attitudes, it is important to be able to assess whether or not this change has occurred, and to what degree. This is the same principle that was discussed earlier in this book in relation to individual learning objectives, namely that there needs to be some form of **measurement** involved. In terms of measuring an overall training programme, this is where the process of **evaluation** is important.

Evaluation is a detailed and sometimes contentious topic, evidenced by the number of contrasting definitions of evaluation which have been put forward over the last three decades –

"Any attempt to obtain information (feedback) on the effects of a training programme, and to assess the value of training in the light of that information."

Source Hamlin, A.C. (1974) *Evaluation and Control of Training*
McGraw-Hill Publishing Company

"The assessment of the total value of a training system, training course or programme in social as well as financial terms. Evaluation differs from validation in that it attempts to measure the overall cost benefit of the course or programme in social as well as financial terms."

Source Manpower Services Commission (1981) *Glossary of Training Terms*
The Stationery Office

"Evaluating systematically looks at the results of the training, notices the differences it has made and determines its value according to pre-set measures. These results are used as feedback to refine the training."

Source O'Connor, J. & Seymour, J. (1994) *Training with NLP*
Thorsons

The latter definition is probably the best of the three, as it discusses pre-determined measurements and acknowledges the cyclical and ongoing nature of the training process.

Who needs to be involved?

Evaluation needs to involve three key stakeholders within the training process –

- The **learner**, in terms of how well he/she has understood and met the learning objectives for the training programme.

- The **trainer**, in terms of the learner's views on how the training was delivered.

- The **organization** or business, in terms of the benefits and costs of the training in relation to the original learning needs which instigated the training programme in the first place.

This approach could open up an extremely broad range of topics and provide a huge amount of information. The key thing is to evaluate aspects of the training which can be acted upon directly by the trainer or the organization. If something is beyond their control or beyond the scope of the original learning needs, it should not be evaluated.

Levels of evaluation

The classic method for determining levels of evaluation is the **Kirkpatrick** model (1967), which identifies four levels of evaluation –

- **Reaction**
  What the learners felt about the event in terms of the delivery of the training.

- **Immediate**
  What the learners actually learned as a result of the training. This can incorporate a process of **assessment**.

- **Intermediate**
  The impact of the training on the learner's job performance.

- **Ultimate**
  The impact of the training on the performance of the organization or business.

There is a fifth level of evaluation which takes place during the training itself, sometimes referred to as **live** evaluation. This is covered in the next chapter on **Communication & Feedback**.

In terms of the stakeholders discussed in the previous section, the **reaction** and **immediate** levels of evaluation are relevant to the learner and the trainer, and can be carried out immediately after the training or shortly afterwards. The **intermediate** level is concerned with the relationship between the learner and the organization, and is carried out at some point after the training takes place. The **ultimate** level of evaluation is focused on the relationship between the organization and the trainer, is generally conducted after the other levels of evaluation, and asks whether the training met the learning needs and whether or not it needs to be continued, changed or cancelled in the future.

Evaluation tools

There is a wide range of tools available for evaluating a training programme, some of which focus on quantitative data (facts and figures), some on qualitative information (feedback, opinions and feelings), and others on both. **Table EA-1** below summarizes the main tools.

Table EA-1 Main tools available for evaluation

Quantitative	Qualitative	Both
• Financial performance • Activity metrics • Tests and examinations	• Interviews • Customer surveys	• Observation • Learner questionnaires • Organization questionnaires • Performance appraisals • Senior management feedback

Which evaluation tools should be used?

The choice of tools will depend on the level of evaluation being undertaken, as discussed in the previous section. Learner questionnaires and interviews are the most commonly used tools for reaction and immediate level evaluation, performance appraisals and activity metrics will often be used to evaluate the intermediate aspects, whereas financial results and customer surveys are often the ultimate evaluation tool for an organization.

Your decision as to which evaluation tools to use will also be driven by your role in relation to the learners and organization, and by time and cost considerations.

If you are a manager or in-house trainer, you will be in a position to take a relatively long term view of training in terms of evaluating its impact on the learners and the organization. You will also be directly accountable for this impact. If, on the other hand, you are an external consultant brought in to deliver a training programme at the request of an organization, your focus is more likely to be on the immediate impact of and reaction to the training from the learners. The longer term impact may determine whether or not you are retained or re-engaged by the organization, but accountability does not necessarily rest on your shoulders.

Time and cost considerations are also important. Interviews and observations are extremely good for collecting detailed information, but they can be time consuming and costly given that each will often involve one-to-one interaction between the learner and the trainer or manager. Learner questionnaires can be risky in terms of the quality and consistency of information collected, but they tend to be relatively inexpensive, quick and if properly designed, highly effective.

Questionnaires

Evaluation questionnaires are generally used with learners immediately or shortly after a training session, with the aim of evaluating two main aspects –

- The **delivery** of the training, i.e. the reaction of the learner.

- The **learning** achieved by the participant in terms of the learning objectives of the training, i.e. the immediate outcome.

Questionnaires can also be used to gain feedback on other aspects of the training such as the training environment (location, room layout, climate etc), but this should only be done if the trainer can directly control these factors in future sessions.

Some rules of thumb for writing questionnaires

An evaluation questionnaire can take a variety of forms, but there are a number of good practices which will help you to make the most of this tool –

- Keep it **short**, ideally a single side of A4 and definitely no more than two sides on a single sheet of paper. The main thing on the minds of your participants at the end of a training course (apart from your closing comments) will be getting out of the training room and going home, so the evaluation questionnaire needs to be brief and straightforward.

- Include **clear instructions** at the top of the page on how the questionnaire should be completed, and how it will **benefit** the participant and future learners.

- If you are looking to assess the learning of individual participants, add a space for their **name** at the top of the page. However, anonymous responses are often the most truthful, so if your aim is to gain general feedback on learning outcomes and the delivery of the training, make this section optional or simply do not ask for the participant's name.

- Include the **date** as a pre-printed section on the form. At the end of a long day people tend to forget or ignore this section, and if you are running multiple or repeat sessions you need to identify which group of learners have completed which set of questionnaires.

- Start with questions designed to evaluate the **delivery** of the training. People like to be asked for their opinions and feedback. If someone has had a positive or negative experience they generally like being given the opportunity to share it or feel that they can do something about it. Also, make the first question **interesting** and relatively **broad ranging**, or people may be disinclined to complete the questionnaire in full.

- Questions designed to evaluate **learning** should be included after the delivery questions, and they should relate directly to the learning objectives for the session. The responses to these learning questions can also provide some illuminating feedback on the delivery and structure of the training programme. If the majority if participants fail to demonstrate successful achievement of a learning objective (i.e. they all get the question wrong), there is likely to be a problem with the way in which that part of the training has been designed or delivered.

- One good way to obtain consistent evaluation information in a limited space is to use a **rating scale** for each question, especially for delivery questions. The usual convention is to use a tiered or numbered rating scale with one end representing the best/highest rating, and the other representing the worst/lowest rating. As a rule, a rating scale should always be based on an **even numbered scale** (for example, 1 to 4). Odd numbered scales often result in the majority of responses defaulting to the middle rating (for example, 3 or 'average') because it is the easiest and least offensive course of action.

- As with learning objectives, evaluation questions should focus on a **single specific aspect** of the training. Avoid branching in questions, for example 'What did you think of the style and content of the presentation slides?' Is the learner providing feedback on the style, the content or both?

- If you are using a rating scale, try to provide space after each question and at the end of the questionnaire for **additional comments**. This will provide information which you may have ignored or originally regarded as unimportant when you designed the questionnaire.

- Finally, at the end of the questionnaire remember to say **thank you** to the participant for taking the time for provide an evaluation.

Review questions

Bearing in mind your own experiences in planning and delivering training, or perhaps referring to a training session in which you have been recently involved, consider how you would answer the following questions.

1   How would you define the process of evaluation?

2   Which evaluation tools did you use in your most recent training event?

3   How did you decide on which tools to use?

4   What would you do differently in the future in terms of evaluating a training session?

5   What are the hallmarks of a good evaluation questionnaire?

Summary

- **Evaluation** is concerned with the measurement of an overall training programme, with the aim of improving the future design and delivery of the same event.

- Evaluation needs to involve three key stakeholders within the training process – the **learner**, the **trainer** and the **organization** or business.

- There are four classic levels of evaluation – **reaction**, **immediate**, **intermediate** and **ultimate**. Evaluation can also take place as feedback during the training session itself.

- The choice of evaluation tools depends on the **level of evaluation** being undertaken. **Learner questionnaires** are the most common tool for reaction and immediate level evaluation.

- Learner questionnaires should elicit feedback on the **delivery** of the training and the **learning** achieved by the participants.

Communication & Feedback

Listening skills
Memory
The feedback process
Feedback questions
NLP in training

Listening skills

Listening is one of the most common and important things that we do. Recent research on work behaviour suggests that we spend approximately –

- 9% of our time writing

- 16% of our time reading

- 30% of our time talking

- and **45% of our time listening**

Listening is also a fundamental part of training and learning. As a trainer, it is important to understand the listening process, have an awareness of barriers to listening effectively, and learn how to listen actively.

Listening as a process

Hearing and listening are not the same thing. In fact, hearing is just the first of **three** stages in the listening process, all of which are fairly obvious but still worth remembering –

- **Hearing**
  Simply the process of sound waves being transformed by our brains into impulses.

- **Attention**
  Important so that we can hear what is being said to us, but often difficult due to distractions such as noise intrusion or internal distractions such as thinking about something else rather than what is being said.

- **Understanding**
  This is the most crucial aspect of the process on a number of levels. As well as understanding what is being said, we need to try to understand the context of the message, and understand the significance of any verbal or non-verbal clues from the speaker. Having a degree of background knowledge regarding the speaker or the subject is also helpful.

Barriers to listening

In most situations there are a number of obstacles which can stop us from listening effectively, and as a trainer it is important to appreciate what these obstacles are and how to overcome each of them.

Broadly speaking, there are **four** types of barriers to listening –

- **Psychological** barriers, including **prejudice, apathy** or **fear** on the part of the listener. For example, someone working in marketing or production may not be as interested in a presentation on annual financial results as an accountant or sales director, given that it may not directly impact on their day to day activities.

- **Physical** barriers, including **disability, fatigue** or **poor health** on the part of the listener. For example, trying to listen to a speaker for long periods while you are suffering from a heavy cold is a fairly difficult thing to do.

- **Environmental** barriers, including distracting **noises**, uncomfortable or poorly positioned **seating**, or an unsuitable **climate** such as an overheated, stuffy meeting room.

- **Expectation** barriers, such as anticipating a **mundane** or boring presentation, expecting to receive **bad news**, or being spoken to in confusing **jargon**.

The trainer can certainly address tangible barriers such as environmental factors or physical obstacles. Dealing with internal barriers can be more difficult, but a lot of this can be achieved by thorough preparation and by designing a training session which will appeal to a variety of learning styles.

Active listening

In order to understand the concept and value of **active listening**, it is worth considering it as one of three different types of listening –

- **Competitive listening**
  You will see this most often in negotiation situations, or when politicians are debating with each other. The person being spoken to is more interested in getting their own point of view across when the other person stops speaking, rather than acknowledging what they have just heard. Alternatively, they are distracted by thinking about their own argument or point of view rather than listening properly.

- **Passive or attentive listening**
  This is always a danger in lecture style presentation sessions. An audience will pay attention to the slides and listen carefully to the speaker, but there is no real opportunity to interact. This means that the speaker may not know how well their message is being understood.

- **Active listening**
  This is the best way to listen for and understand the real message in what people are saying. It involves taking the next step from just listening attentively, by looking to show obvious interest in what the speaker is saying, and by trying to interact with them. As a trainer you need to try to use active listening yourself, and provide opportunities for learners to use active listening techniques as well. This is of particular importance when involved in informal training activities such as coaching and mentoring.

In terms of outlining the techniques which can be used for active listening, it is useful to think back to the three basic stages of the listening process – hearing, attention and understanding.

- **Hearing and attention**
  - → First and hopefully obviously, **stop talking**.
  - → Try to eliminate as many **distractions** as possible, both external and internal.
  - → Try to control your own **non-verbal signals** to the person speaking. This could mean paying attention to your physical stance, your body movements, eye contact with the speaker, and encouraging motions such as nodding or smiling.

- **Understanding**
  - → Make sure that you understand the **purpose** of the speaker, and also be aware of you want from the conversation.
  - → It also helps to take **notes**, but try to focus on writing down key words and phrases that will jog your memory later, rather than trying to write down everything that is being said in an act of dictation.
  - → If possible, try to ask **questions**. You can use the notes you have written to remind you of points that need clarification. Try not to interrupt though!
  - → Finally, try to use the technique of **reflecting** what the speaker says to you.

Reflecting

This is a technique used extensively by people involved in consultative selling, but it is also a very useful tool for trainers. Communication can be broken down into three levels – facts, thoughts (or beliefs) and feelings (or emotions). Reflecting works on all three levels –

- Repeat the **facts** that you think you have been given by the speaker. This is sometimes referred to as 'parroting'. If you are right, you know that you are getting the basic elements of what the speaker is telling you. If you have made any mistakes, this gives you both an opportunity to get back on to the same page.

- Also share the **thoughts** or **beliefs** that you have heard, and try to convey the underlying **feelings** or **emotions** which you believe are involved. For example, the speaker may be very upset and wants you to display empathy or sympathy with their situation. It is this reflection of thoughts and feelings which distinguishes reflecting from just parroting back to the speaker, which might get a bit tedious and annoying for all concerned.

Again, this is a very useful tool when coaching or mentoring. It can also be used during feedback sessions in a more formal training environment.

Listening game

Try this quick quiz as an icebreaker with your colleagues in a meeting, or to illustrate the difficulty of effective listening. Read the following passage to your group –

- Go to the left luggage locker number 252 at St. Pancras station. In the locker you will find a cash box, which contains the following: fifty-two £1 coins, ten 50p coins and twenty 10p coins. Please bring me twenty-five £1 coins, two 50p pieces and all of the 10p coins. What is the number of the locker?

- Provide the group with four possible answers: 522, 255, 252 or 525.

- If most people get the answer wrong, it is probably because they were more concerned with the amounts of money involved and the directions being given, rather than the locker number. This may be due to their expectations about what was going to be asked, or a failure to take notes during the reading of the passage.

Memory

Memory is an intrinsic part of the learning process. Without delving too deeply into the science of memory, brain activity is controlled by neurons, which are linked by pathways. As a pathway is used more frequently, it becomes stronger. This means that memory is an **associative** process. In other words, the more you can associate a piece of information with a previous experience, the more likely you are to remember it. This is another reason why **experiential learning** is such a powerful tool for adult learners.

As with the listening process, **attention** is an important factor in supporting effective memory. Other factors include **motivation**, our **emotional state**, the **context** in which the information is presented, and the **environment** in which the learning is taking place.

There is an old three step maxim regarding lectures and presentations, along the lines of 'tell them what you are going to tell them; tell them; tell them what you have told them'. This may be a bit simplistic, but it is based on the principles of **primacy** and **recency** effects. This means that memory is strongest at the start of a training session and at the end. In fact, recency tends to be stronger than primacy, so whilst first impressions are important, it is the way in which a training session ends that can have the greatest influence on a group of learners.

These principles can also be applied to the component parts of a training programme. By dividing the session into manageable parts, and reviewing the learning at the end of each part, the learning process is usually enhanced. Evaluation questionnaires at the end of a training session can also play a useful role in reinforcing learning and improving memory.

The feedback process

Feedback is the process by which learning, listening and memory are all brought together. It can also make the difference between an average training programme and an exceptional one. There can be pitfalls to giving and receiving feedback, but adopting a structured approach and remembering a few simple rules can help you to use feedback in a productive and motivating way.

Figure CF-1 below provides an outline of the feedback process.

Figure CF-1 The feedback process from the perspective of a trainer

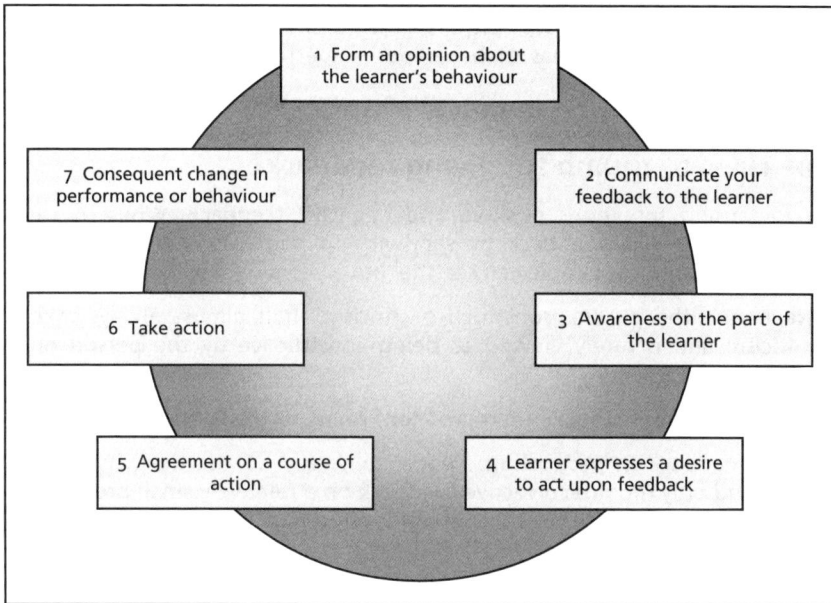

As mentioned above, there are some common pitfalls at each stage of this process, and each pitfall can have a compounding effect on subsequent stages –

1   **Form an opinion about the learner's behaviour**
    Opinions can often be biased or influenced by personalities, culture or prejudice.

2   **Communicate your feedback to the learner**
    The feedback can be given in the wrong way, at the wrong time or in the wrong environment. The classic example is criticizing someone's performance or behaviour publicly in front of their peers.

3   **Awareness on the part of the learner**
     The feedback may be rejected or ignored by the learner.

4   **Learner expresses a desire to act upon feedback**
     The learner feels that the feedback is wrong or irrelevant, or the feedback is too general to identify a specific learning need.

5   **Agreement on a course of action**
     The learner may find it difficult to apply the feedback to a practical course of action, perhaps due to a lack of relevance to their work situation.

6   **Take action**
     The agreed action fails to take place due to a lack of supervision, motivation or relevance.

7   **Consequent change in performance or behaviour**
     As a result of previous pitfalls, the desired change fails to occur. Alternatively, other areas of behaviour or performance begin to suffer as result of this action.

Some rules of thumb for giving feedback

- Avoid using the terms **positive** and **negative** feedback. Whilst it can be tempting to give feedback by sandwiching negative comments between positive ones, most people can see the 'but...' coming from a mile off.

- Never use the phrase 'constructive criticism'. It is almost always taken as criticism and is rarely viewed as being constructive by the person on the receiving end.

- Try to think of feedback in terms of **confirming** or **correcting** behaviour.

- Keep feedback in **proportion**. People generally do the majority of things well, and only require corrective feedback on a relatively small proportion of their activity. Levels of feedback should reflect this. Praise often and publicly, and correct privately.

- Feedback should be **timely**, and given during or immediately after an event.

- Feedback should be **specific**, otherwise it will come across as general criticism or a general acceptance of certain behaviour or performance levels.

- Ask for **permission** to give feedback. This way, the other person is consenting to the process and is more likely to respond positively.

- Focus on **behaviour** and not attitudes. This avoids personalizing feedback, which could cause resentment on the part of the recipient.

- Explain the **benefits** of a change in behaviour, either for the individual or for the organization.

- Agree an action plan and a timescale, and stick to it. Whilst it is important to frame feedback in a positive manner, there must also be **consequences** for action or a lack of action.

Feedback questions

Feedback should be an integral part of any good training programme. The key to doing this well is to **prepare** your feedback sessions during the design phase of your training programme, both in terms of how and when the feedback will take place, and what the feedback is likely to cover. The real trick is to make a feedback session appear natural and organic to all of those participating, whilst remaining in control of the direction of the session and relating it to the learning objectives.

One way to do this is to prepare a series of feedback questions in advance. You may not use all of them during a feedback session, but they will give you a structure around which you can plan the discussion. Broadly speaking there are three types of feedback question –

- **Recall questions**
  Designed to help learners recall knowledge and experiences.
  These can include –
  → Describing (Describe what/how…)
  → Observing (What happens when/if…?)
  → Listing (Name…)
  → Identifying (What is…?)
  → Matching (What other…?)

- **Process questions**
  Designed to help learners to understand specific processes or methods involved in learning.
  These can include –
  → Distinguishing (How would you distinguish 'a' from 'b'…?)
  → Comparing (What do 'a' and 'b' have in common…?)
  → Analyzing (Why did/would…?)
  → Grouping (What is similar/the same as…?)
  → Explaining (How did…?)

- **Application questions**
  Designed to help learners to apply these processes or methods.
  These can include –
  → Applying (What would happen if…?)
  → Forecasting (Based on 'a', how could…?)
  → Speculating (In this particular situation, what would happen if…?)
  → Inventing (How could 'a' be used…?)

These questions can be customized to fit a particular topic, and can be selected on the basis of the specific learning objectives for that topic. For example, if the learning objective is to apply a concept to a real life situation, an application question would be the most appropriate selection.

NLP in training

Neuro Linguistic Programming (NLP) is a framework for modelling how people interpret and respond to information received through each of their five basic senses. Its origins are in behavioural science research from the 1970s, but NLP has since grown into an extremely lucrative industry in its own right, with applications ranging from training to business management. It is important for a trainer to have an appreciation of what NLP is, and how it can relate to a training programme, without necessarily trying to acquire a detailed knowledge of the entire methodology. In other words, be aware of what it is, just in case anyone asks you!

NLP is primarily concerned with the **state** of the learner, in terms of their thoughts, emotions, behaviours and physiology. From a training perspective, NLP can help to move a learner or group of learners from their current state, which may not be conducive to learning, through to a desired state. For instance, this is why icebreaking activities are so popular with trainers, helping to relax participants or break down preconceptions.

With its emphasis on state via the learner's senses, NLP has direct relevance to some of the learning intelligences discussed in the **Training Basics** chapter, in particular **visual**, **linguistic** (auditory) and **kinesthetic** (physical).

There is a whole range of presuppositions within NLP, but the key one is that everyone lives within and operates from their own model of the world. No two people are alike, and this is something of which every trainer should be aware. Different people learn in different ways, and different people may be successful in the same task due to different ways of approaching that task. In essence, NLP can provide a methodology for many of the processes and techniques described throughout this book. However, a thorough understanding of NLP is not a prerequisite for understanding these processes and techniques. If you would like to learn more about NLP, some further reading is recommended at the end of this book.

Review questions

Bearing in mind your own experiences in planning and delivering training, or perhaps referring to a training session in which you have been recently involved, consider how you would answer the following questions.

1   What are the three stages of the listening process?

2   What are the main characteristics of active listening?

3   How can you design your training event to maximize a learner's memory of what you cover?

4   What are the main pitfalls which can occur when giving feedback?

Summary

- **Listening** is one of the most common and important things that we do, and it is a process based on three stages – **hearing, attention** and **understanding**.

- There are four types of **barrier** to listening – **psychological, physical, environmental** and **expectation**.

- The most effective form of listening is **active listening,** based on showing obvious interest in the speaker and trying wherever possible to interact with them.

- **Primacy** and **recency** principles can help to improve the memory of learning.

- Try to think of **feedback** in terms of confirming or correcting behaviour rather than simply positive or negative. Keep feedback **timely, specific** and in **proportion**. Focus on **behaviour,** not attitudes.

- There are three types of feedback question – **recall, process** and **application** questions.

- **Neuro Linguistic Programming (NLP)** is a useful technique for understanding and managing the state of learners. The key presupposition is that everyone lives within and operates from their own model of the world, and training should take this into account.

Tools for Training Activities

Problem solving techniques
Motivational techniques
Icebreakers

Problem solving techniques

Earlier in this book we discussed the importance of experiential learning for adults, and the relevance of **problem solving** as a training method for these learners. Group activities are a good way to break up a training session, and an excellent way for learners to share experiences and solve problems. As a trainer it is important to maintain a level of control over group activities, and to provide learners with tools and direction to help them move towards their learning objectives.

One of the most commonly used problem solving methods is **brainstorming**, which is an effective way of encouraging every member of the group to share their ideas and experiences, and requires relatively little preparation on the part of the trainer except for providing a flipchart or whiteboard and some pens. However, the strength of brainstorming is also its main weakness – it can be a fairly unstructured activity, and as such can be difficult to manage from a training perspective, especially if a relatively small number of group members dominate the discussion.

There is a range of problem solving techniques which can be employed in a group work environment to help maintain a sense of direction, timing and structure to the activity.

Brain writing

There are a number of variations on this technique, but in essence **brain writing** is a more structured version of brainstorming. It is based on each group member writing or drawing their ideas on a piece of paper, and then passing the paper on the member sat next to them and repeating the process until everyone has written three ideas on each piece of paper.

This technique is sometimes referred to as the **6-3-5 method**, given that the most common structure is to have six pieces of paper and six group members, each of whom will write three ideas on each piece of paper, with five minutes allowed for each set of ideas. These figures can be changed depending on the size of the group and the topic under discussion, so for instance you could have four people writing two ideas on each piece of paper in two minutes. It is important to limit any verbal communication within the group until the cycle of ideas is completed.

Brain writing is particularly useful for encouraging equal participation from every member of the group. It is also good for developing ideas, as a member can read some of the previous ideas which have been written down, and add any suggestions or amendments. However, it can become a little tedious once you come towards the end of the cycle, especially if people start to run out of ideas or simply duplicate ones already written down. This is where good facilitation on the part of the trainer is important. Brain writing is often a useful precursor to a traditional brainstorming session, where the ideas collected can be discussed openly by the group. It may be that the trainer decides to bring the activity to a close before the cycle is completed, and begin a discussion instead.

SCAMPER

This is a good technique for stimulating fresh ideas when a group has reached something of a dead-end in trying to solve a problem. **SCAMPER** is a checklist of active verbs defined by **Robert Eberle** which can be applied to any problem or situation –

- Substitute
- Combine
- Adapt
- Modify
- Put to another use
- Eliminate
- Reverse

A group can apply some or all of these actions to a problem, and then discuss the ideas which develop. For example, a group may have been given the problem of improving the performance of a car. They may decide to substitute petrol for another fuel, or a traditional combustion engine for a lightweight rotary engine. On the other hand, they may consider eliminating certain elements such as rear seats, or adapting the rear windscreen into an air deflecting spoiler.

This can become a bit of a free for all, or a group may rely too heavily on just a couple of the actions, so it is important for the trainer to facilitate this properly. One good way is to allocate sets of actions to a member or members of the group, and then collate the ideas in a brainstorming session afterwards.

The Concept Fan

This technique is sometimes a bit more difficult for groups to understand or for a trainer to facilitate, but it can be incredibly useful, especially for visual and logical learners. The Concept Fan is a creative thinking technique devised by **Edward de Bono** (1992). It is based on generating alternative ideas for a problem, and displaying these in a diagram. A whiteboard and/or adhesive note pads are best for this activity. The note pads are particularly useful because they can be moved around without wiping and rewriting ideas.

The Concept Fan works by taking a step backwards from a problem to find a broader idea or concept, and you keep taking steps backwards from the original problem until you have produced enough alternative ideas, some of which may prove useful and some of which may be discarded.

The classic example used by De Bono is the problem of attaching an object to the ceiling, and discovering that you do not have a ladder available to help you to achieve this. **Figure TT-1** below provides an example of how the Concept Fan could be used to provide alternative solutions to this problem.

Figure TT-1 Example of solving a problem using the Concept Fan

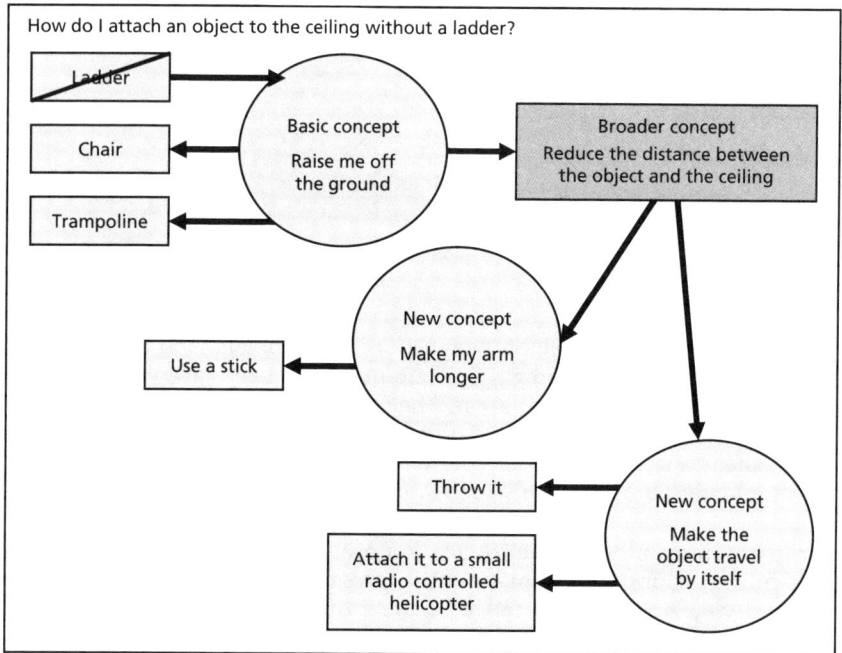

The first stage is to establish the **basic concept**, which in this example is raising yourself off the ground in order to reach the ceiling. This could open up alternatives such as using a chair or, if you are feeling a little more creative, a trampoline! If none of these alternatives are available, the next stage is to take a step backwards and establish the **broader concept** behind what you are trying to do, in this example reducing the distance between the object and the ceiling (in other words, raising yourself off the ground is just one way of achieving this broader aim). This could then open up other more interesting possibilities such as trying to make your arm longer or perhaps even making the object travel by itself up to the ceiling!

This technique does tend to generate some fairly unusual and occasionally silly ideas, but this is what makes it so useful for creative or lateral thinking activities. Once a group has started the process of drawing the diagram and discussing increasingly exotic ideas, the activity requires minimal facilitation (unless things get too out of hand). If you are using a whiteboard it is also a good way to get the group out of their chairs and on their feet.

Assumptions

Most problems and decisions involve one or more assumptions, many of which are taken for granted or ignored. However, assumptions are a valuable and often essential part of the problem solving process. For example, a **project** is a structured way of solving a problem or achieving a goal. A project manager needs to include a set of assumptions when creating project plans so that everyone involved in the project or its end result is working towards the same goals within the same constraints. In other words, they are all on the same page should any further problems arise.

As well as providing shared constraints and guidelines, **stating the assumptions involved in a problem** can also be a good way of starting to deal with the problem itself. Whilst many assumptions are the result of circumstances beyond our control, others may well be result of preconceptions or are simply self imposed.

Self imposed assumptions can include –

- **This problem has to be solved within a certain timescale.**
  Is the timescale self imposed, is it internally imposed or is it imposed by external influences such as customer requirements?
  Would adjusting the timescale enhance or reduce your chances of solving the problem?
  Are you in a position to change the timescale?

- **We have always addressed this problem in this way.**
  Why has this problem always been addressed in this way?
  Is this the best way to deal with this particular problem?
  Has there been a change in circumstances since the problem last occurred?
  Are you able to change the approach to solving the problem?

- **The solution to the problem exceeds the budget.**
  Is the budget the most important factor in deciding how or indeed whether to solve the problem?
  Will other factors such as revenue growth or customer satisfaction outweigh the budget constraints?
  Can you change the budget?

- **If we cannot solve the problem we will have failed.**
  What is your definition of failure?
  In whose eyes will you have failed – your own, your team, your manager or your customer?
  How does the problem fit within the wider scheme of things, both internally and externally?
  Are you in a position to decide or influence what does and does not constitute failure?

- **It is impossible to solve the problem.**
  Is it impossible in your opinion?
  Does everyone involved share this opinion?
  Is it impossible due to physical or technical constraints?
  Would development or investment address these constraints?

By listing and questioning the assumptions involved in your problem, you may well find a number of previously unseen solutions. On the other hand, it may become clear that the problem cannot be solved or is not worth solving due to the impact on other areas or activities.

Reframing and the Four Ps

How often have you used or heard the phrase '*Let's look at this from a different perspective*' or '*Let's try to look at this from someone else's point of view*'? This simple approach to problem solving can be given a more formal framework by using the **reframing** approach, and it can be an extremely useful technique in training and workshop sessions. This idea was initially developed by **Michael Morgan** in his book *Creating Workforce Innovation* (1993).

There are many ways to reframe a problem, but one of the most effective is to create a reframing grid or matrix, and to place different perspectives on a problem or situation into each part of the grid. As with the **concept fan**, a reframing grid appeals to people who like to adopt a visual or logical approach to problem solving. It is also a very good way to structure a **brainstorming** session, with ideas or questions categorized as being from one of a number of perspectives. **Figure TT-2** on the next page illustrates a basic outline of a reframing grid.

Figure TT-2 Outline of a basic reframing grid

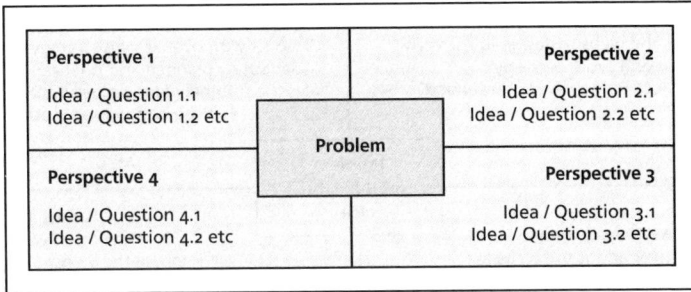

Perspective 1		Perspective 2
Idea / Question 1.1 Idea / Question 1.2 etc	**Problem**	Idea / Question 2.1 Idea / Question 2.2 etc
Perspective 4		Perspective 3
Idea / Question 4.1 Idea / Question 4.2 etc		Idea / Question 3.1 Idea / Question 3.2 etc

The next question is how to categorize or define different perspectives. Again, there are many ways of doing this and it often depends on the nature of the problem, or the type of situation in which the problem has arisen. In a business situation, the **four Ps** approach is a well established method of reframing a problem.

The four Ps approach is based on determining whether each of the following is right or wrong, working or failing, requires some form of change, or whether it is meeting the needs of customers or users –

▪ Product

▪ Planning

▪ People

▪ Potential

For example, imagine that you are delivering sales training to a small business which has set up a new website to market and sell their products online, but they are not seeing the anticipated or forecasted levels of orders from customers. Reframing this problem using the four Ps could help you to find one or a number of solutions, as illustrated in **Figure TT-3** on the next page.

Figure TT-3 Example of using the Four Ps with a reframing grid

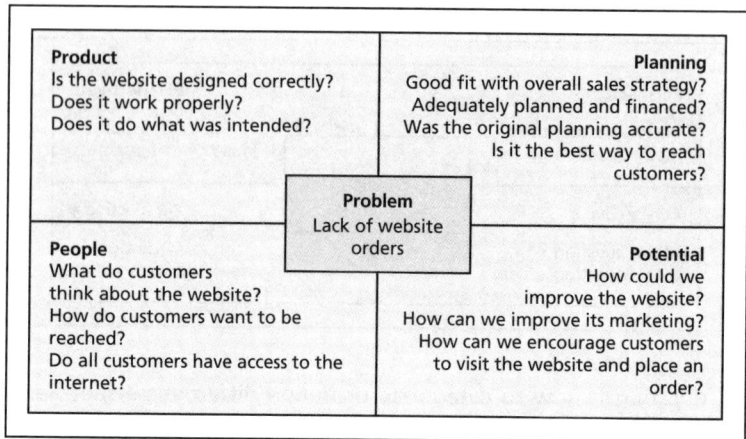

Product Is the website designed correctly? Does it work properly? Does it do what was intended?	Planning Good fit with overall sales strategy? Adequately planned and financed? Was the original planning accurate? Is it the best way to reach customers?
Problem Lack of website orders	
People What do customers think about the website? How do customers want to be reached? Do all customers have access to the internet?	Potential How could we improve the website? How can we improve its marketing? How can we encourage customers to visit the website and place an order?

This approach usually provides a broad and detailed range of potential solutions, and can be used to involve all stakeholders internally (for example sales, marketing, design and IT) and externally (including customers and key influencers). It may also highlight shortcomings and strengths within specific aspects of a business or project.

Force and PESTLE Analysis

In addition to looking at the problem itself, it is often helpful to look at the **forces** acting upon a particular problem, be they forces of change, influence or power. These forces can be listed and then evaluated to determine which ones have a positive impact and which have a negative impact. In other words, which forces may help to solve the problem and which could make it worse.

Force field analysis

This problem solving technique is sometime referred to as **force field analysis**, and can be used to structure a brainstorming session. Force field analysis simply involves listing forces acting upon a problem or situation as either being positive (driving forces) or negative (restraining forces).

General forces to consider may include –

- Costs

- Benefits

- People

- Relationships

- Resources

- Interests

- Structures

- History

- Policies

- Values

By listing specific examples of these forces as positive or negative, you can then start to evaluate each one in terms of its relevance, strength, impact and your ability to change or use each one. A simple rating system (1 to 5 or 1 to 10, with 10 as strong and 1 as weak) is a good way to do this. The relative scores of the positive and negative forces may help you to decide how to solve the problem, or whether it is actually feasible to solve the problem.

PESTLE analysis

There are many variations on the concept of force analysis. **PESTLE analysis** is used to look at broad ranging influences acting upon a problem, with the PESTLE mnemonic representing –

- **Political**
  For example, the influence of government on your problem or your ability to influence government with regards to the problem.

- **Economic**
  General economic factors such as share prices, exchange rates or interest rates, and the impact of these on the problem; local or regional economic factors; unemployment levels; labour costs; income levels.

- **Social**
  This could include the impact of cultural factors, public opinion, lifestyle choices or religious considerations.

- **Technological**
  Your problem may be solved or exacerbated by technological developments or constraints, or perhaps by the cost implications of a technological solution.

- **Legal**
  For example, regulations, legislation or taxes which could impact upon your problem or any planned solution.

- **Environmental**
  This may incorporate legislative factors or ethical dimensions.

This framework can be useful for dealing with problems which have strategic or ethical implications. Clearly, different societies and geographical regions will have different considerations to look at when using a tool like PESTLE, and may well reach different solutions to a particular problem. You may also see this framework referred to as PEST, STEEPLE or SLEPT.

Motivational techniques

This section is designed to provide a practical and accessible introduction to the often complex topic of **motivation**, and suggest how motivational techniques can be applied to a training event or workshop session. After all, if your participants are not motivated during a training programme, they are unlikely to meet the learning objectives and even less likely to benefit from the experience.

Why is motivation important?

Whether you are trying to achieve something yourself or lead others towards an achievement, the ability to be self-motivated or to motivate is crucial. When we meet people who are regarded as successful or high achievers, it is tempting to assume that they are innately self-driven, or are natural leaders with high levels of motivational ability. This may well be the case, but it is just as likely that they have learned and used some effective techniques for either motivating themselves or to motivate others.

The benefits of motivation to an individual are fairly obvious – people who are motivated tend to be more successful in achieving their personal and professional goals, which in turn has benefits in terms of their self-esteem and confidence. Given that people are usually the most important asset of any organization, motivation is also a critical factor in the overall success of a team or business.

Three golden rules of motivation

Motivation does not take place on its own. In order to be motivated or to motivate others, it is important to remember three golden rules of motivation before considering any specific techniques.

1   **Motivation is impossible without clear achievable goals**

Motivation and goal setting are inextricably linked. Without a goal or purpose, motivation is meaningless, whilst motivation is a vital part of intentionally achieving any goal. Two of the most basic motivators are to know exactly what you are trying to achieve, and to then go out and achieve it. Not having a clear idea of your goal or not believing that a goal is attainable·will severely dent your motivation.

2   **Motivation and goals need to be in alignment at every level**

How often have you felt that you have been performing well or doing a good job, only to be told by your manager or colleagues that you have been focusing on the wrong thing, that priorities have changed or that you have simply been underperforming? For example, imagine an experienced sales person who has an excellent track record of retaining business with their established customers, but is heavily criticized by their manager for failing to develop as much new business as their less experienced colleague. As a result, the sales person feels alienated, undervalued and ultimately de-motivated. Their performance and results are likely to suffer. The chances are that there has been a lack of dialogue between the manager and the sales person over how individual goals need to fit with the overall goals of the company. If the emphasis is on generating new business, has this been communicated effectively to each sales person, and in a manner which will motivate each of them to succeed?

Every business needs motivated employees in order to be successful and achieve its goals. If employee motivation is not closely matched to these business goals, the chances of success are diminished.

3   Motivation is neither fixed nor infinite

Motivation is not a one-off event. Something which provides motivation at one particular time may not be as effective in the future, due to changes in environment and circumstances. If someone is driven to become the best in their field, how do they maintain their motivation to perform once they reach the pinnacle of their profession? Even if circumstances remain constant, the most powerful motivational factors will lose impact over the course of time. For instance, you may attend a conference and feel energized by a particular speaker or meeting, and leave the event highly motivated to put what you have heard into action. How long will the impact of what you heard last before you slip back into old ways of doing things?

Motivation is a constant process and constantly changes. As an individual or as a leader trying to motivate others, it is vital to remember this.

Setting effective goals

At this stage it is worth remembering some basic rules about setting goals. In order for a goal to be effective, regardless of the context in which it is being set, it should follow each of these five **SMART** rules –

- Each goal should be as **specific** as possible. The more general a goal, the less meaningful it is and the less likely you are to achieve it.

- It needs to have some form of **measurement**, so that you know to what extent it has been achieved.

- Any goal involving teams should be **agreed upon** by each person involved in setting the goal and trying to achieve it. If it is a personal goal, you are effectively agreeing a contract with yourself to see the goal through to the end.

- Goals should be **realistic**, although this does not necessarily mean that they should be easy. In fact the best goals generally stretch you into reaching new standards of achievement or performance. If there is no prospect of achieving something, it is not likely to provide motivation.

- Finally, your goal should be **time-based**. In other words, there should be a fixed point at which you will determine whether or not the goal has been achieved.

For example, simply saying *'I want to know more about motivation'* may be a laudable ambition but it is not a particularly good goal. A SMART goal would be something along the lines of *'after reading this chapter, I will be able to list five motivational techniques'*. It is based on a specific task, you have a specific number of techniques to list, you have decided to do it so you have agreed upon a course of action, it is realistic given that the work involved is simply reading this chapter, and it is time-based because it should be achievable on completing the chapter.

Each of these SMART factors will help your goals to provide effective motivation – you should know exactly what you are trying to achieve, be able to determine how well you have done it, agree upon the goal with your manager or made a personal commitment to do it, believe that you can achieve the goal if you make the necessary effort, and know when the goal has been achieved.

From a training perspective, asking your participants to prepare SMART goals for the session, either before they arrive or as part of your introduction to the event, will help them to 'buy in' to the whole process and provide some form of self-measurement at the end of the training.

Motivational theories

There are a range of established theories which underpin many popular ideas about motivating other people and motivating yourself. This next section provides a brief overview of five key theories relating to motivational drivers, self awareness and interaction with others –

- Maslow's Hierarchy of Needs

- Herzberg's Motivation-Hygiene Theory

- McGregor's X-Y Theory

- McClelland's Achievement-Motivation Theory

- The 4-D Theory of Behaviour

Although there are arguably some flaws within a couple of these theories, each is of value and may help you to better understand how to motivate yourself more effectively and how to motivate your training event participants.

Maslow's Hierarchy of Needs

Figure TT-4 Maslow's Hierarchy of Needs

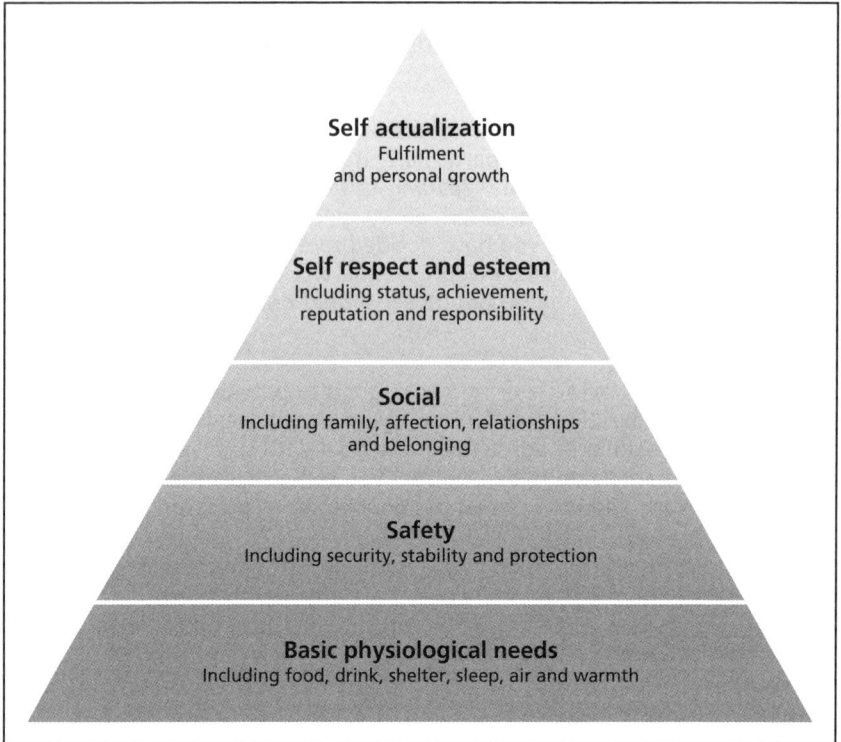

This classic model of self-motivation was put forward by **Abraham Maslow** in 1943, and is based on a pyramid of ascending basic motivational drives as illustrated in **Figure TT-4** above. It is based on the idea that once a person has achieved their needs at one level, they then move up a level and are motivated by more sophisticated types of need. The limitations of this model are fairly obvious – the most basic needs are often the strongest motivators, and are usually constant. Also, different people will place a different emphasis on each type of need, and will react differently when these needs are met. Remember the third golden rule – motivation is neither fixed nor infinite. However, Maslow's original framework does provide a useful starting point and an easy to understand model.

Herzberg's Motivation-Hygiene Theory

Sometimes referred to as the Two Factor Theory, **Herzberg** (1959) identified two types of factor in the workplace which either lead to job satisfaction (**motivation** factors) or job dissatisfaction (**hygiene** factors). The term hygiene may seem a little odd, but it basically means that the factors leading to dissatisfaction are usually associated with things that are expected to be in place as part of the *status quo* but which are not necessarily viewed as motivators in themselves. For example, factors such as salary, working conditions, management style and relationships with colleagues can all de-motivate if an individual is unhappy with them. If there is not a problem, these things tend to be taken for granted and may not be viewed as being obviously motivational.

Herzberg argues that motivating factors which lead to increased job satisfaction tend to be intrinsic to the role itself, and are based on attitude motivation rather than motivation through tangible incentives. These motivation factors include having a sense of achievement, recognition for these achievements, the nature of the role or activity, having responsibility, opportunities for career progression and the prospect of personal growth. All of these can be strong motivators for participating in a training programme.

There are also weaknesses in the motivation-hygiene theory, not least because it tends to assume that all de-motivating factors are external rather than being driven internally by the individual concerned. However, its strength lies in the emphasis on personal motivation and qualitative rather than quantitative factors. In other words, this theory suggests that rewards and salary are not always the best answer. It is fair to say that these incentive based factors certainly will not work on their own if more intrinsic factors relating to the role are not addressed, often through learning and professional development.

Mcgregor's X-Y Theory

If Maslow and Herzberg are the most established models of analyzing self-motivation, **Douglas McGregor's** X-Y Theory (1960) is one of the most well known models of motivational management. The theory contrasts two opposing styles of management –

- **Theory X** refers to managers who lead through direction, targets and sometimes even coercion. It is based on an assumption that most people dislike work and will try to avoid performing at their maximum unless directed otherwise. This approach can lead to intolerance, insecurity and an inability to delegate. Responsibility is rarely shared, but it is the team that is ultimately accountable for failure.

- **Theory Y** describes a more inclusive management style based on encouraging participation through delegation, and is based on the assumption that work is a natural activity and not something to be avoided.

Rewards based on achievement are more effective than punishment based on failing to act upon instructions. Responsibility is shared but accountability rests with the manager.

Few people would argue against Theory Y being the more appropriate approach towards motivating a team to perform at their best. The danger is that any manager can slip into Theory X behaviour if they are driven by short term business goals, such as achieving tough quarterly sales targets, or are being managed themselves by a Theory X manager. Anyone working in a sales environment is likely to have experienced these pressures – many sales organizations are aware of the need to adopt an inclusive approach to managing their employees, but the overriding priority is always to hit the numbers. How often have you heard a manager say that they would like to adopt a more inclusive, long term approach to developing their team but are constantly distracted by 'firefighting'?

Of course, just as Theory X is generally undesirable, Theory Y is often impractical to adopt in its entirety. The key is to strike a balance which addresses critical short term business goals with the longer term organizational goals of employee development and motivation, both of which can be addressed to a large extent through training.

McClelland's Achievement-Motivation Theory

Another theory of motivation which applies to both employees and managers is the **acquired needs theory** developed by **David McClelland** (1961), which suggests three basic needs which drive everyone in the workplace –

- **Achievement** motivation, referred to by McClelland as **n-ach**. It is based on the achievement of goals and feedback from others confirming this sense of achievement.

- **Power** motivation (**n-pow**) based on the need to direct others, influence strategy and sometimes to acquire increased personal prestige.

- **Affiliation** motivation (**n-affil**) based on interaction, support and team membership.

No individual person will have only one of these needs, but will possess a mix based on varying levels of each motivator. McClelland argues that achievement is the most effective motivational factor, especially for managers and leaders, and this has resulted in his ideas being referred to as **achievement-motivation theory**. The idea of achievement as the primary motivator also fits in with the first golden rule of motivation outlined earlier – motivation is impossible without clear **achievable** goals. The emphasis on achievable is important bearing in mind the SMART rules of **goal setting**. The importance of achievement as a motivator should have a bearing on how you measure and reward activity during a training event, even if it is simply certificate of achievement at the end of the programme.

The 4-D Theory of Behaviour

At the start of this overview of motivational theories, we explored Maslow's idea of an ascending hierarchy of needs, and criticized the notion that the most basic human needs such as physiological, safety and security factors were left behind once they had been fulfilled. Recent research by **Nitin Nohria** and **Paul Lawrence** (2002) suggests that these fundamental human drives continue to motivate our behaviour, even within the workplace. They summarize their ideas as the 4-D theory of human behaviour, based on four key motivational drives –

- The drive to **acquire** resources and rewards (D1)
- The drive to **bond** with others (D2)
- The drive to **learn** and **understand** (D3)
- The drive to **defend** against threats from others (D4)

Nohria and Lawrence argue that the most effective types of motivation address each of these four basic drives in equal measure, and should also be applied to the ways in which organizations manage their business and their people. These four drives can also apply to training, both in terms of individual motivations to participate and the organizational motivation to initiate the training in the first place.

Icebreakers

Starting a training event with a long period of formal presentation can often be intimidating and challenging for learners, and stressful for the trainer. It is also counter intuitive when the basic principles of adult learning are considered, namely the importance of experiential learning and group interaction. This is where **icebreakers** can be a useful and enjoyable way of opening a training session, or energizing a group after a break or at the end of a long day.

There is a huge range of icebreaking activities available, many of which can be found by browsing one of the major online search engines. The CIPD website also has a good range of activities. Bearing in mind all of the aspects of training which have been discussed in this book, two things are worth considering when planning an icebreaker –

- Try to keep any icebreaking activities relevant to your group size, group background and training topic. Explain to the group why you are asking them to participate in the icebreaker, whether it is to help them learn more about their fellow learners, develop their problem solving skills, or just to relax and have a bit of fun!

- Keep the activities as simple as possible. If they require a large amount of preparation they are likely to detract from the main focus of the session. If they require a large amount of explanation to your learners, the activity may cause confusion, distraction or frustration, which will defeat the object of the exercise. The aim is to make participants comfortable, relaxed and ready to get involved in the next part of the training event.

Here is a selection of icebreakers designed for helping participants to get to know each other at the start of a session.

True and false

- Give each group member a piece of paper and a pen.

- Ask them to write the following on the page – their name, and in no particular order two facts about themselves which are true and one fact which is false.

- Encourage the group to be as outrageous as they can with all three facts (within reason). Ask them to consider topics such as hobbies, achievements etc.

- Swap the pieces of paper between the group members, and then ask each person in turn to read out the information on the page, starting with the author's name.

- The author says hello to the group, and then their fellow learners try to guess which of the three facts is false.

- This is a good way of getting the group to interact and to learn a little more about each other. The chances are that many of the true facts will be more outrageous than the false ones!

- It is usually a good idea for the trainer to join in as well.

Rogues' gallery

- This requires a little more preparation on the part of the trainer. Before the start of the training session, ideally during a welcome period with tea and coffee, take a photograph of each group member with an instant camera. Alternatively, ask each participant to provide a photograph before the event takes place.

- Stick the photographs on a noticeboard or whiteboard, arranged in groups of three or four people. If you cannot get hold of photographs, just write their names in small groups. Also, some people may be uncomfortable with having their photograph taken.

- Ask the participants to break out into these small groups, either during the welcome period or in the training room.

- Ask each group to find out one or two facts about each other, such as a favourite hobby, special moment or proud achievement.

- Each group then reports back to the rest of the participants, with each member discussing one of their colleagues.

- This is another good way of getting people to interact and find out a little about each other, without the element of blatant exaggeration and bluffing!

Line-up

- Divide the participants into groups of five to ten people, and ask them to stand in a line one behind the other.

- Each group is then asked to put themselves in order according to a category given by the trainer, such as shoe size, height, name, time spent with the organization etc.

- This becomes more interesting (and sillier) if you ask them to do this without speaking!

- This icebreaker is good for getting people out of their seats and moving around, and as such is just as useful after a long presentation session or a lunch break.

Further information on training

If you would like to know more about training techniques or training as a career, an excellent first place to look is the official website of the Chartered Institute of Personnel and Development at **www.cipd.co.uk**

For further reading on training skills and theory, you may want to consider the following books –

Hackett, P. (2003) *Training Practice* CIPD

Bee, F. & Bee, R. (2003) *Learning Needs Analysis and Evaluation* 2nd edition CIPD

Honey, P. & Mumford, A. (1992) *The Manual of Learning Styles* Peter Honey Publications

Gardner, H. (1993) *Frames of Mind: The Theory of Multiple Intelligences* Fontana

O'Connor, J. & McDermott, I. (1996) *Principles of NLP* HarperCollins

De Bono, E. (1992) *Serious Creativity* HarperCollins

There is also a vast amount of material available via the internet on every aspect of prescribing, planning, delivering and evaluating training.

For more learning resources on training, project management, sales skills and personal development please visit the my-skills website at **www.my-skills.co.uk**